The Grief and Memory WorkBook

"At the blueness of the skies and in the warmth of summer, we remember them."

~ Sylvan Kamens & Rabbi Jack Reimer

How to Use This Book:

This workbook is designed by therapists, to help you store essential memories of someone that you loved, but have lost, and process your feelings at the same time.

We recommend that you take your time, and fill this in slowly. Do not rush through. If you are finding things too painful, please stop and put this away for a while. Writing things down can be a healing process, and we hope by the end you will have been able to process some of your emotions around your important person.

Please take care with the last section, and please do not start before you feel ready. If you are having trouble processing grief and loss over time, it may be important to have a chat to a professional.

Remember: You can keep your person alive in your heart, while also 'living' your life.

Section 1:
The Important Details of My Person

Name: Nickname?
Date of Birth/Birthday:
Age When Passed Away:
How Long Ago was That?
What was your relationship to them?

Section 2:
What Were They Like?

What did they look like? (Height, hair/eye color, other features etc.)

What was their personality like? (Funny, loud, caring, organized etc)

What would make them laugh?

What upset them?

What rules or routines were important to them? (i.e. Taking shoes off inside)

Did they ever get embarrassed or anxious?

Did they have any bad habits?

Did they have a favorite?...
Food

Flower

Vehicle

Style of Clothing

Location

Drink

Color

What sort of Music/TV Programmes/Movies did they enjoy?

What other activities did they enjoy?

Section 3:
What Happened in Their Life?

Where did they live most of their life?

Where did they go to school? What was that like for them?

What was their childhood and family like?

What did they do in their life? (Career, family etc.)

Did they have any pets?

What else?

Section 4:
You and Them

Where and when did you meet?

What did they call you?

What activities would you do together?

What are some of your earliest memories of them?

Do you remember some big events (good or bad) that you experienced together?

Did any events make them particularly happy?

Did you ever discuss any big decisions with them? What sort of advice did they give?

If you knew they could drop by and visit tomorrow, what would your ideal day spent together look like?

"I'll be seeing you

In all the old familiar places

That this heart of mine embraces

All day through."

~ Billie Holiday, I'll Be Seeing You

Section 5:

Handle with Care Questions

What did you love about your person?

What do you miss the most?

What did they struggle with in their life?

Not all memories we have of someone we loved are nice ones, are here any hard things you would like to write here?

Is there anything you wished you had said before they passed away?

Is there anything you would like to say about when/how they passed away?

How do you think they have impacted your life?

What advice do you think they would say to you right now?

Do you have something physical to remind yourself of them?

How will you honour their memory?

After all these questions, how are you feeling? What will you take forward with you into the rest of your life?

Anything else you would like to include? Stories, drawings etc.

Section 6:
Some Self-Care Ideas, Challenge Yourself to Try Something New........

Talk to an old friend
Visit someone
Organize a 'Special Day Out'
Exercise/Lift Weights/Boxing
Yoga, Tai Chi, Pilates
Buy your favorite ice-cream
Go for a walk/hike
Sit or lie down outside
Get a haircut/die your hair
Build something/Take something apart
Try a new hobby/craft/class
Go on or plan an adventure
Go and watch a sports game
Meditate or pray
Write a letter
Do something fancy
Take your (or your friend's) dog for a walk
Join an online group
Visit the library
Bird Watching
Watch a funny movie/videos
Research something you are interested in

Play music loud
Play board games/cards/video games
Do something arty/crafty
Create your own website
Go to the beach
Find some things to sell
Read a magazine/buy a new cookbook
Write a poem or diary
Give someone a hug/ask for a hug
Gardening
Paint your nails
Have a bubble bath
Make a list of goals
Write a list of all the good things in your life!
What else can you think of?

Printed in Great Britain
by Amazon

22727018R00020